Prese

MW00674367

From:

Date:

---

www.listentolife.org

Listen to Life
Like a Child

and make a life,
not just a living.

Toll FREE 1-877-4DRJOEY
www.listentolife.org

ISBN 0-9715074-2-2

Library of Congress Control Number: 2005904033

FIRST EDITION

Toll FREE 1-877-4DRJOEY
www.listentolife.org

I dedicate this book to God, the Author of Life, without whom I would be silent and to our daughter, Rebekah, who leaves our home and goes to college this fall. The world awaits your stories, Scooter. Show us God. Our lives depend on it.

Toll FREE 1-877-4DRJOEY
www.listentolife.org

Contents

"Hold My Hand"
Listen to Life for God   31

"Be Good"
Listen to Life with Your Hands 59

"Look Both Ways"
Listen to Life with Your Attitude 79

"Play Nice"
Listen to Life with Your Spirit   106

Order the *Listen to Life* Series Today!

Listen to Life
Like a Child

and make a life,
not just a living.

Toll FREE 1-877-4DRJOEY
www.listentolife.org

The Beginning of the Beginning

Once upon a time, in a land that may seem far, far away, you were a child. Not just a little adult. You were a child.

And as hard to believe as it might be for you, you heard "Love You!" so much each day that it may have been one of the first sentences you spoke. You listened to your life with your heart.

And not only did you listen to life with your heart, you listened to life for God. Every time you reached up, there was a hand for you to hold. And each time you held a hand, it was like holding the hand of God.

So with a heart full of love and a hand held by God, you found it relatively easy to be good and to use your hands to be good to others. You treated others like you wanted to be treated and were somewhat mystified when some kids didn't.

Well, as a good child, rooted by your heart full of love and guided by God's hand, your attitude was positive and realistic. You learned that cars run over even good boys and girls when they walk out in the street without looking both ways. So you decided it was best to look both ways not just at intersections of streets, but at crossroads in life. Other children were different from you, but that was okay because they were kids, too. You looked both ways, not just your way.

So with your attitude looking both ways, your heart overflowing with love, and God's hand holding and guiding you down the good paths of life, your spirit jumped for joy when it was playtime. You knew that to enjoy playtime, you had to play nice. So you did and shared your love, and held the other kids' hands, and treated them the way you wanted to be treated, and always looked both ways before crossing the street.

Then something happened. You grew up. And you decided that you couldn't be a child anymore. That you had to act grown up. And so you left behind your lessons learned and sat at the feet of a new teacher. This new teacher taught you that revenge is stronger than love, and only the weak hold hands. You learned that good is relative so get all the goods from your relatives and friends that you can. You bought the lie that attitude is supposed to strike fear in the hearts of your competition and since life is a competition, playing nice is for sissies. So you bottled up your spirit and said, "Lead or get out of the way, because I'm coming through."

But now something else has happened to you. The new teacher's lessons have left you joyless, restless, and heartless; distressed, dissatisfied, and despairing; unhappy, uncomfortable, and uncaring. You don't enjoy playing by the new teacher's lesson anymore, just making a living. You know there's more, but where? You want to make a life, but how?

Please know that you're not alone.

Your story is my story. That's how I know your story so well.

And that's why I wrote this book. I found myself in a critical, spiritual condition that affected me physically, mentally, emotionally, and socially. I chose not to just make a living, but to make a life. My pathway of healing and wholeness was to become a child again.

Now don't think for a second I just sat down and thought of this one day. I wish I were that smart, but I'm not. I learned it from our daughters. I observed that listening to life like a child was the road to making a life, not just a living when my wife and I had our two daughters, Rebekah and Elizabeth. At first, I saw them as projects, little adults to be shaped and molded into mirror images of my wife and me. Pretty soon though, I figured out these two incredible girls are their own persons with indomitable spirits and that I could learn a great deal from them. The roles were reversed. The students became the teachers. And I discovered the joy of listening to life and making a life, not just a living.

My journey took a decided turn down, all the way down to becoming a child again. Not to being childish, even though I am sometimes, but child-like. There's a huge difference and you'll discover it through these strategies and stories.

Each section of this book represents a mile marker for me, a set of lessons or strategies that keep me moving forward each day toward listening to my life like a child and making a life, not just a living. I want to share them with you because, well, that's what children do when something good happens to them—they share the goodness, knowing in some innate way that by sharing it, the goodness multiplies.

And that's my prayer for you: that your goodness multiplies.

That you become once again the incredible, beautiful, marvelous, wonderful child that God created you to be. That you listen to your life like a child and make a life, not just a living.

So have fun reading this book! Don't get in a big hurry with it, either. Each strategy/story is short enough for you to read pretty quickly, but the goal here isn't to finish the book. Your mission is to allow yourself to be transformed by God. That's why there are three "Listen to Your Life" reflection items after each one. Some are questions. Some are activities. All of them are oases for your journey, places where you can sit down, think, feel, discern your spirit and God's Spirit, and discover what God is up to with you. But transformation of your life—learning to listen to life like a child and make a life, not just a living—is the destination.

You'll probably ask more than a few times, "Are we there yet?" That's okay. You've traveled far, far away from the land of once upon a time when you were a child. Getting back takes a while. Moving forward isn't all that easy. But, man, is it worth the trip!

So be kind to yourself. Don't expect too much. Just enjoy the journey. And you might want to take along a companion. Get a friend or two a copy of this book and share the journey. Having someone to travel with helps the time pass and it keeps you accountable for reading, reflection, and rewards.

And thank you so much for letting me journey with you. You bless me by inviting me along.

Have fun!

"Love You"
Listen to Life with Your Heart

"Love You!" Just think about all of the times you've heard or said those two words. When your mother kissed your forehead before she walked out of your classroom on the first day of school, she said, "Love You!" And I'll bet you said "Love You!" to your child on the first day of school, too.

When your father walked you down the aisle or escorted you as your best man on your wedding day, he kissed your cheek or hugged you with tears in his eyes and said, "Love You!" And I'll bet if you haven't yet, you'll do the same thing one day.

Ever been with a loved one or friend in the holding area outside of a hospital operating room? Whether you're horizontal or vertical, those last words are "Love You!"

Stood over a casket lately with a lump in your throat, and whispered, "Love You!"?

"Love You!" punctuates all of these life experiences, reminding you where to breathe God's love. Sometimes you inhale, because your love saturation level is low. Other times, you exhale, because someone else is dizzy without love.

But what about everyday kind of life experiences? You know, the kind of life events in which "Love You!" surprises you; the mundane minutia that seems trivial by comparison and yet, from the midst of it, emerges God's love.

Children don't wait for "big events" to say "Love You!" They listen to life from the heart. And you can, too.

Here are eight strategies and stories about children that coach you to listen to life like a child from your heart.

"Love You!"

Strategy 1: Write a Love Note

I knew the next day would be a busy one as I went to bed that night. It was one of those "I'd better sleep fast" nights because my schedule was overflowing for the next day. In fact, as I thought about it, I knew the whole week would be that way. You've been there, I'm sure—consumed with how in the world you'll get everything done while you're trying to go to sleep. Your mind racing around, "I'm only one person!" and "Where can I save some time tomorrow?"

Well, after rolling around the bed that night, I got up the next morning and packed a lunch, knowing that I wouldn't have time to eat out and would have to work straight through just to get a good jump on things. My wife had made her delicious chicken salad so I made a sandwich out of it and cut a slice of apple pie. I'm scurrying around the kitchen, "getting it done," when our younger daughter walked up and said, "Daddy, do you want me to get you a lunch bag?"

I said, "Sure, sweetie...thanks."

Later that day, when it dawned on me that it's time to eat, I opened my bag, reached in, and expected to take out my sandwich. Instead I pulled out a note, in my daughter's hand-writing, that read, "Dear Daddy, Don't work too hard today. I love you!"

That love note totally transformed my attitude. I relaxed, realizing that I didn't have to do a week's worth of work in a day, and enjoyed my lunch. I kept the note and still have it in one of my desks today. I open the drawer when I'm feeling rushed and read that love note...and listen to life and make a life, not just a living.

Listen to Your Life

1. How do you typically react when you have more to do than humanly possible?

2. When my daughter took her lunch to school, I regularly wrote her love notes and put them in her lunch bag. That's how she learned the power of a love note. When was the last time you wrote someone a love note?

3. If God wrote you a love note today, what would it say?

Strategy 2: Be Grateful for Loving Acts You Don't Remember

Do you remember your mother and father getting up at two a.m. to feed you?

Now I didn't ask you if you remember getting up to feed your child at two o'clock in the morning. I asked you if you remember when you were an infant lying in a crib, screaming your head off because your stomach is growling, and all of a sudden, this bleary-eyed person appears over your crib, reaches down, picks you up, and holds you close. You feel the warmth of that embrace. You hear a soft voice. You are fed. And the next thing you know, you fall asleep again, back in your crib, totally satisfied and happy. That's what I'm talking about. Do you remember that experience?

Of course not. Even though it happened night after night for quite a while, depriving your parents of much-needed sleep, you don't remember those gracious acts of compassionate kindness your parents offered just because they loved you.

But even though you don't remember them, it doesn't mean they didn't happen. And because they happened, you can be grateful for them even though you don't remember them.

There is probably no way you can remember all of the gracious acts of kindness others have done for you out of love. Some of them you don't even know about. Prayers offered for your safety as you drove away from your home for the first time.

A diaper changed. A sippy cup of juice poured. Long hours worked to buy you new jeans or pay car insurance.

You can be grateful for these loving acts even though you don't remember them. All of these acts combine to make you who you are today—a wonderful, unique human being trying to listen to life and make a life.

Listen to Your Life

1. If your parents are living, call them and thank them for the sacrifices they made for you like feeding you at 2:00 a.m.

2. If your parents aren't living, write them and express your gratitude for their loving acts. Keep the letter handy and read it regularly.

3. Make a list of other loving acts of kindness your parents probably did for you, but you don't remember. Thank God for each loving deed.

Strategy 3: Listen to Life for Love

A mother who listens to life through our web site at www.listentolife.org emailed me with a story about the time she and her three-year-old son were playing with their cat, Smokey. Smokey was purring very loudly, enjoying all of the attention and obviously quite happy.

The mother said, "Listen to Smokey's motor running," referring to the loud purring.

Her son quickly said in that sweet three-year-old language, "That not her motor running. That God in her heart!"

Then the mother said, "Cats purr because they're happy and loved and you're right, she's happy because God's love is in her heart."

And then her son said, "Just like me!"

Now every time she hears a cat purr, she thinks about God's love in their hearts, and in her son's. And, she says, in hers.

Do you listen to life for love? So what reminds you of God's love being in your heart? What makes you purr with happiness?

Listen to Your Life

1. When was the last time you sat down with someone you love—like this mother with her child—and just played?

2. What gets your motor purring with an awareness of God's love?

3. When your motor stalls out, how do you get purring with God's love again?

Strategy 4: Request a Song on the Radio for Someone You Love

It was my birthday. It started normally enough. I'm in the bathroom shaving, like I do every morning, with the radio playing a local station. (One that airs my syndicated radio show, of course.) I'm feeling pretty good about celebrating another year of blessings.

All of a sudden, the announcer came on, gave the call letters of the station, and started playing a phone interview…with our younger daughter. She told him that it was my birthday and asked him to play a song in my honor. He asked her how old I am and she told him. Then he asked if she'd get in trouble for telling my age. "No sir," she said.

"What song do you want me to play for your daddy's birthday?" the announcer asked.

And she said, "Buddy Jewell's song, *Help Pour Out the Rain (Lacey's Song)*."

Now you may be wondering, "Why that song?" It's about a father who listens to life while driving his daughter to school. She wants to know if when she goes to heaven, she can help God pour out the rain.

Well, about that time my daughter showed up in the bathroom door and I'm standing there all teary-eyed, and we hugged, and I told her, "I love you. Thank you for a great birthday present!"

So often we walk through the malls and department stores,

strip centers and super stores, looking for a birthday present that says "I love you." And yet so often, the best way to say "I love you" is to just listen to your heart and never spend a dime. Just do something like request a song on the radio for someone you love. And not just any song, but a special song like Buddy Jewell's song is to me. Now that's making a life, and not just a living!

Listen to Your Life

1. What's a birthday present that someone gave you that said, "I love you"?

2. Now think about one of the most meaningful birthday presents you ever gave. Where did you find it, more specifically the idea for it?

3. What did that gift cost you, not just financially?

Strategy 5: Love and Let Live

Around holidays like Thanksgiving, most Americans get together with family members to share a meal and some time together. Of course, it's been since last year when you saw these family members and for some of us, that's by choice. I mean, you can choose your friends, but you can't choose your family. You're just kind of lumped together by birth. Which means being family can be a real challenge sometimes.

Knowing that being family can be a challenge, a teacher discussed the Ten Commandments with her class of five and six year olds. She explained the commandment to "honor your Father and your Mother." Then she asked the class, "Is there a commandment that teaches us how to treat our brothers and sisters?"

Without missing a beat, one little boy, the oldest child in his family, answered, "Thou shall not kill."

Love isn't just an emotion. It's a choice. Sometimes you may feel like killing a family member. (Not really, but you know what I mean.) But you choose to love and let live, just seeing that person as swimming in the same gene pool with you, but uniquely different and that's okay. You don't have to change that person or get rid of him or her. When you listen to life and make a life, not just a living, "love and let live" is a choice you make.

Listen to Your Life

1. I suppose we all have at least one family member who is challenging to be with. Who's yours?

2. Why? What does that person do or say that makes you want to change him/her?

3. See yourself choosing to "Love and Let Live" with regard to that family member. How did you do it?

Strategy 6: Always Leave a Hug

Pam, who listens to life with us on her local radio station and at www.listentolife.org, sent me an email about some friends who adopted a baby from China. They named her Abbie. Abbie is so precious and a joy to everyone she meets, and especially to her mom and dad.

Well, one day Abbie's mom left to go shopping without Abbie knowing it. You know the trick—the ole "Mommy sneaks off shopping when the toddler's not looking so the toddler won't get separation anxiety" trick commonly known as, "out of sight, out of mind."

But Abbie was smarter than that. She realized her Mommy was gone, and asked her Daddy, "Daddy, where's Mommy?"

And her Daddy said, "Abbie, Mommy has gone shopping and will be back soon."

Abbie said, "Well, I miss her."

And her Daddy said, "She'll be back soon."

And Abbie said, "I know, but she forgot to leave my hug."

There's just something special about a hug, isn't there? Hugs give us something to hold on to until we can be together again.

Now I know what with harassment lawsuits prevalent at work and sexual innuendo woven into our everyday fabric, you may be wondering, "Yea, but is it safe to hug anymore?" I know some hugs offered from some people are inappropriate so be careful, but these few misuses and oversensitivity cause us to overreact to the point where we hardly touch at all anymore. This lack of touch leaves us isolated and lacking intimacy in our daily lives.

So listen to life and hug. It's a vital part of making a life, not just a living because you share God's love when you hug. Ask before you hug if you're unsure and respect the other person's wishes. But especially remember—always leave a hug at home.

Listen to Your Life

1. Who did you hug last? Why did you hug? How did that hug feel to you?

2. Look around you. See anyone who needs a hug? How can you appropriately ask and offer a hug to that person?

3. The next time you feel isolated or lacking intimacy, close your eyes, take three deep breaths, and imagine God hugging you.

Strategy 7: Let God Be Proud of You

I stood in-line at a restaurant with some friends, placed my order, moved away from the counter to get a table and waited for my food to arrive. As I stepped toward a table, I passed by the others who were waiting in line. And one guy in particular caught my eye.

He was smiling, but not just any smile. I mean an ear-to-ear, face-splitting, I'm-so-happy-I-could-laugh-for-no-reason-at-all smile. And I wondered, "What's he so happy about?"

And then I looked down and saw why. He was holding a baby carrier. I knew immediately that he must be a new daddy.

"Congratulations," I said. "Boy or girl?"

"A girl," he said, and swung the carrier around for me to see.

"How old is she?" I asked.

"Five weeks old today," he said, still smiling that huge grin.

"She looks like the prettiest, smartest little girl ever born," I told him.

"She is," he beamed.

Is there anyone in the universe prouder than a new parent? Which is kind of odd when you think about it—that child has done nothing but be born and didn't do that all by herself. She's been trouble since she was born, disrupting her parents' sleep patterns, causing them to adjust their every priority and desire to put her needs first, and just generally causing chaos and mayhem in the home. And she hasn't even smiled the first time!

Yet this father is the proudest man in the restaurant. Why?

Because his pride in her isn't rooted in her doing anything. His pride in her is because she belongs to him. She is his daughter.

Just like this new father, God, your heavenly Father, is that proud of you; smiling all over creation not because of anything special you've done, but simply because you are a child of God.

Do you ever find it difficult to let God be proud of you? Maybe because you remember all your disappointing even harmful acts? God's proud smile over you isn't based on your perfection, but on your relationship with God. You are a child of God. And that means God loves you!

So listen to your life for birds singing, gorgeous rainbows, beautiful sunrises, and all of the other expressions God creates to smile over you. Make a life, not just a living by letting God be proud of you!

Listen to Your Life

1. Remember when your children were born. How big was your smile? Or, if you're not a parent, talk with a friend who is about how proud they were when their children were born.

2. How do you best sense God's proud of you—through nature, music, friends, poetry, or what else?

3. God's smile over you is a spiritual resource you can renew daily. Doing so helps you remember that God is proud of you for who you are, not just for what you do. Choose something you can experience daily from #2 above to remind yourself of God's unconditional love.

Strategy 8: Love without Looking

Our younger daughter and I were buying some roses for her school principal. I picked up the prettiest pink roses we could find, held them out to her, and asked, "How do they smell?"

She took a deep breath, and said, "They don't."

"What do you mean, 'They don't,'" I said. And I smelled them, and she's right—they don't.

So we started sniffing around through the roses and found that none of them really had a fragrance. And, of course, our daughter asked, "Daddy, why don't they smell?"

"I don't know," is all I could come up with.

"Well, your roses smell good, Daddy," she said.

"Yes, they do," I said. "But mine don't look as good as these."

"True," she said, "But I know you love me without having to look at your roses. I can just smell them from anywhere in the house."

I guess looks aren't everything, are they? When you can walk around your home and smell the love, you realize that looks aren't all that important anyway.

But the truth is—most of us base our love on looks. We look at someone and faster than we can blink an eye, we decide by that person's appearance whether or not he or she is someone we can love.

If you're really intentional about listening to life and making a life, not just a living, this last strategy of "Love You!" is critical. To love another for who she is, not for how she looks is the most important step in your spiritual growth to becoming a more loving person. Suspend your judgment for a blink or two or three hundred times, and love without looking.

Listen to Your Life

1. When you're working on a project around your home and realize that you require something from the hardware store, do you clean up before you go? Why? And how much?

2. The next time you see someone for the first time in a while, become aware of your first reaction. Ask yourself, "What did I just do in reacting to seeing this person? And did I love without looking?"

3. How do you want others to love you? And how do you want God to love you?

"Hold My Hand"
Listen to Life for God

Children look for a hand to hold, don't they?

As a preschooler, when I couldn't breathe due to an asthma attack, and it was 3:00 a.m., and I thought I was going to die from lack of air, and my head was light and I was passing out, there was a hand to hold.

When I went to kindergarten for the first day and wasn't at all sure about why I was there or had to go and sure didn't want to leave my Mama, there was a hand to hold.

On a Sunday morning, as the congregation sang, "I am resolved no longer to linger…" and I knew I had to come out of that pew and go down that aisle to give my life to God forever, and I was still scared because what if I failed God, but when I went down that aisle anyway, there was a hand to hold.

As a fifth-grader, I left the familiarity of my all-white school to go to the east side of town, across the tracks, and I was scared when they herded us out of the building and onto the buses because of a bomb threat, but the buses didn't move, they remained parked at the school, but then, right there in the midst of Southern racial conflict screaming in the face of integration, there was a hand to hold.

Children don't wait until someone offers a hand. They reach out and take a hand. So does God. God reaches out and takes your hand in all the times of your life and doesn't wait for you to reach out first.

Here are thirteen strategies and stories about children to coach you to listen to life like a child and make a life by looking for God's hand everywhere.

Strategy 1: Pray Before Every Trip

Our family got in the car for a short trip one weekend afternoon. We all buckled up and as I backed out of the garage, our preschool-aged daughter said, "Daddy, we forgot to pray." We always hold hands and pray before going on a long trip.

"This isn't a long trip, sweetheart," I said.

"Daddy, we've got to pray," she insisted.

"All right, we'll pray," I said. And so my wife and I held hands, and reached into the backseat, where we each held one of our daughter's hands.

Twenty minutes later when we arrived, our daughter said, "I told you it was gonna be a long trip, Daddy. It just seemed shorter because we prayed."

Are their some trips in your life that you think you can handle on your own? I suppose we all fall prey to a case of the spiritual terrible-two's—"I can do it!"—at some point in our life journey. We delude ourselves into believing that we are self-sufficient, independent, self-made women and men who exist separate from the need of Godly intervention or blessing.

At such times in my life, even the short trips became miserably long. But when you pray, like our daughter, you discover that all the trips seem shorter because God travels with you.

Hold God's hand during all of your trips and pray as you listen to life and make a life.

Listen to Your Life

1. What was your last experience along life's journey when you didn't pray?

2. What do you think you can handle on your own as you travel, something that keeps failing?

3. Hold God's hand, and pray right now, asking God to shorten your trip and give you traveling mercies.

Strategy 2: Find a Place Each Day Where You Can Be with God

A child wandered around the woods near his home. At first his father let him wander, but over time the father began to worry. "The woods are dangerous," he thought. "I don't know what's out there."

So he decided to discuss the matter with his son. One day he took the boy aside and said, "You know, I've noticed that each day you walk into the woods and wander around for a while. And I'm wondering, why do you go there?"

And the boy said, "I go there to find God."

"Well, that's a very good thing," the father said. "I'm glad you're searching for God. But, son, don't you know that God is the same everywhere?"

"Yes," the boy said, "I know God is the same everywhere. But I'm not."

Are you the same everywhere you go? Probably not. Most of us put on different masks, variable identities, Gumby-like personalities according to our situations and who we're with. Going within yourself and being just who you are doesn't happen everywhere.

Do you have a special place you go where you can find God? Whether it's wandering in the woods or a special room in your home or your car or truck, find a special place where you can be who you are before God. Create a holy space in which you can find God and hold God's hand. And where God can stretch out a hand and find you.

If you truly want to listen to life and make a life, not just a living, you must find a place where you can be with God daily, just like you are—no pretension.

Listen to Your Life

1. Observe yourself in different situations. Are you the same in each? What's different about you?

2. Discover an easily-accessible space that is a favorite of yours. A place where you feel peaceful and free to be who you are; a space where you can find God's hand. What can you do to make this space your own?

3. Getting to your new-found space is key. When will you come to this place? How often? Make it a priority in your day. Get up 15 minutes earlier. Or, watch 30 minutes less TV. Somehow, get to this space.

Strategy 3: Ask God to Hand You What You Need

A mother told her little boy, who was very much afraid of the dark, to go out to the back porch and bring her the broom. The little boy turned to his mother and said, "Mama, I don't want to go out there. It's dark."

The mother smiled reassuringly at her son. "You don't have to be afraid of the dark," she explained. "God is out there and will look after you and protect you."

The little boy looked at his mother real hard and asked, "Are you sure God's out there?"

And the mother said, "Yes, dear, I'm sure. God is everywhere, and God is always ready to help you when you need it."

The little boy thought about that for a minute and then went over to the back door and opened it just a little bit, barely a crack. He peered out into the darkness, and said, "God? If you're out there, would you please hand me the broom?"

I'm kind of like that little boy, aren't you? When I'm afraid, I want God to show up and help out.

But how often do you actually ask God to hand you something, believing, as the mother said, that "God is everywhere, and God is always ready to help you when you need it?" More often, you may just become paralyzed with fear, and forget to ask God very specifically to hand you what you need, even something as mundane as a broom.

You see, when you ask for what you need, you declare your interdependence with God. You acknowledge that you weren't created to do life on your own, and that to truly listen to life and make a life, you want God's help.

So, if you want to hold God's hand, ask God for it!

Listen to Your Life

1. What is your dark fear? What are you afraid of?

2. What could you ask God to hand you to overcome this fear?

3. Ask for what you need right now.

Strategy 4: Say to Yourself,
"I Will Live Forever, Just Not Here."

The holidays are a lot of fun and excitement even for us "big kids," but sometimes there's a little bit of sadness for me because I remember all of the family gatherings we had when I was a little boy. Some of those folks I loved so much aren't here anymore. And I can't hug and kiss them or talk with them like I want to at our family gatherings now.

Learning to live with the reality that we live forever, just not all of it here, is difficult at times. We experience it at an early age, don't we? As a three-year-old, my nephew encountered this fact of life for the first time when his great-grandfather, the man he knew as Papaw, died. To help my nephew begin to understand life, death, and eternal life, my brother took him to the funeral home to see Papaw.

"Daddy, who is that?" the little guy asked.

My brother said, "Who do you think it is?"

And my nephew said, "I think it's a big doll that looks like Papaw because Papaw is already in heaven."

Sounds like he's got things pretty well figured out, doesn't it?

One of the reasons holding God's hand is so important is because while life here is a gift from God for you to enjoy, it's not the only gift God has for you. One day, your great-grand-child might stand over what you left behind here and declare it "a big doll." The best way to make that transition from life here to heaven is holding God's hand, to be in a personal relationship with God.

Life here can be hard enough at times. That's reason enough to hold God's hand. Making the transition through death to heaven is something that requires God's hand. You can't make it alone, but then you don't have to. Just reach out and hold God's hand in this life...and the next. That's the best way to listen to life and make a life, not just a living, for an eternity.

Listen to Your Life

1. Who is the first person you remember dying among your family and friends?

2. What events surrounding that death do you recall?

3. Jot down what you hope to leave as your legacy when your life transitions to the next.

Strategy 5: Pray Constantly,
But Especially Ahead of Time

A little girl, dressed in her Sunday best, ran as fast as she could, trying not to be late for worship.

As she ran, she prayed, "Dear God, please don't let me be late! Dear God, please don't let me be late!"

Well, as she was running and praying, she tripped on the curb and fell, getting her clothes dirty and tearing her dress. She got up, brushed herself off, and started running again. As she ran, she prayed again, "Dear God, please don't let me be late. But please don't shove me either!"

I guess we all pray those panic-button prayers, don't we? But not only do we want God's help, we also want to tell God how to help us.

Sure, God wants to hear from you in all the times of your life. One of the advantages of praying ahead, though, is that you generally are more open, or take the time to be open, to what God might want to say to you. You're less directive than you are in panic-stricken situations when you assume you know more than God about what's necessary at the time.

After all, what's the point of praying if you tell God what to do? God becomes a cosmic-sized bubble gum machine in which you insert your prayer, turn the lever with an "Amen!", and hold out your hand to see if you receive the color prize you asked for.

Instead of waiting until you're running behind in life to pray for help, pray today. And instead of telling God how to help you, just ask for help and let God decide what's best. God will let you know by sending you the help you need when you need it. That's how to hold God's hand while you listen to life and make a life, not just a living.

Listen to Your Life

1. Honestly recall your last personal prayer with God (your private, not public prayer.) Was it panic-button or proactive prayer?

2. When you pray, who does most of the talking—you or God?

3. What might God want to put in your hand if you listened instead of just talked?

Strategy 6: Call God When You're Scared

We had just tucked our younger daughter in for a good night's sleep when a thunderstorm blew up. The wind whistled. The lightning flashed. And the thunder rattled the windows. It was a pretty good-sized storm.

I heard all of this sound-and-light show from downstairs in my recliner. Between the "booms" I heard this muffled voice calling, "Daddy! Daddy!" So I went upstairs to her bedroom where I found her with the covers pulled up over her head.

"What's wrong?" I asked.

"I'm scared of the thunder," she said. "Will you lay down with me?"

"Sure," I said as I got under the covers. And putting my head under them, I looked at her the best I could in the dark and said, "But why does it help with me under the covers?"

"Because the thunder can't hurt me when you're here. You're my Daddy," she said.

Do you hear the trust in her voice? Do you feel the sense of security that my presence brought her, that just my being there made a huge difference?

Somehow as a sophisticated, allegedly mature, self-sufficient adult, you might view a declaration of fear as childish, foolish even. And yet those very insecurities prevent you from being honest enough with God about your fears to invite God under the covers of your life.

Who do you call when you're scared by life? (You know you get scared, don't you?) Call your heavenly Daddy, God, and invite God to lie down with you. Life can't hurt you when God's with you. Oh sure, you suffer some, but when you trust God and accept God's presence, life really can't hurt you, because you're holding God's hand.

Or, more importantly, God's holding yours.

Call God and then listen to life as you make a life, not just a living.

Listen to Your Life

1. Remember the last time you were scared. What/Who scared you?

2. Why were you scared?

3. What difference would trusting God and inviting God to be present with you have made?

Strategy 7: Write God a Note

A teacher asked her class to write notes to God. Here are a few:

"Dear God, I didn't think orange went with purple until I saw the sunset you made on Tuesday. That was cool.

"Dear God, Instead of letting people die and having to make new ones, why don't you just keep the ones you have?

"Dear God, I bet it's very hard for you to love all of everybody in the whole world. There are only four people in our family and I'm having a hard time loving all of them.

"Dear God, In school they told us what you do. Who does it when you're on vacation?

"Dear God, Are you really invisible or is it just a trick?

"Dear God, Did you mean for the giraffe to look like that or was it an accident?

"Dear God, Who draws the lines around the countries?

"Dear God, I went to this wedding and they kissed right in church. Is that okay?"

So if you could ask God anything, what would it be?

"Dear God, why did John get that promotion and I didn't?

"Dear God, Susan's daughter always gets the lead in the spring dance. Why not my Debbie?

"Dear God, if you can do anything in the world, why did my mother have to suffer and die such a horrible death?

"Dear God, couldn't you just have stopped Sam from hitting me?

"Dear God, would you please make Christy come back home?"

Write God an honest note. Hold nothing back. God can take it. Ask God to hold your hand as you struggle through your questions, trying to listen to life and make a life, not just a living.

Listen to Your Life

1. Get a clean piece of paper and a pen or pencil.

2. Sit down and write an honest note to God, asking whatever question is important to you right now.

3. Put the note somewhere you'll see it often. Keep the backside of the paper clean so when your answer comes, or the way to live with the lack of an obvious answer comes, you can jot it down.

Strategy 8: Ask God to Clean You Out

It was October. And our family was doing what millions of other families across this fair nation were doing—carving a pumpkin. Our pumpkin wasn't just any pumpkin though. It was a pumpkin that we accidentally grew and thought was a watermelon until it turned orange. (Okay, so we'd never grown a pumpkin before.)

I cut the top out of the pumpkin and then it was time for one of us to scoop out the inside. No one wanted to do it. "It's nasty," said one of our daughters. "It's slimy," said the other. And you know it really is. I mean, have you looked into and felt around a pumpkin lately?

Nobody wanted to do the dirty work of scooping out the pumpkin. So my wife and I did it, knowing that if we didn't, the smell would be unbearable in a day or two of front-porch living.

Like our daughters were about scooping out the pumpkin, I guess we're all like that about scooping out our spirits. Maybe you're not. Maybe you're one of those people who regularly do a moral inventory, examine your behavior and attitudes, and inspect your innermost thoughts.

Most of us don't. Most of us put the lid back on all kinds of slimy stuff we don't want to touch—hatred, greed, anger, jealousy, prejudice.

And then God comes along and says, "I'll do it." God knows your life would be unbearable without the scooping, a smelly mess.

But the only way God can clean you out is if you smile like a jack-a-lantern today and let God scoop you clean. Yes, it may scrape a little, but as with any proficient surgeon, God removes what needs to go and prepares you for healing.

So smile and invite God's hand to scoop you clean as you listen to life and make a life, not just a living.

Listen to Your Life

1. Write down at least a couple of slimy, smelly things inside of you that need to go.

2. Put a big smile on your face and pray, "God, I invite you to scoop me clean of these slimy, smelly character flaws."

3. Prepare to make a better life!

Strategy 9: Be Prepared...for Anything

Do you always get the response you're after? Like when you ask your spouse or your child or a coworker a question? Do you ever get an answer that you just didn't anticipate at all?

One day a first grade teacher was reading the story of Chicken Little to her class. She came to the part of the story where Chicken Little tried to warn the farmer. She read, "...and so Chicken Little went up to the farmer and said, 'The sky is falling, the sky is falling!'" The teacher paused, and then asked the class, "And what do you think that farmer said?"

One little girl raised her hand and said, "I think he said: 'Holy Mackerel! A talking chicken!'"

The teacher couldn't teach for the next ten minutes.

You probably have heard that story so many times that you take the details for granted, like a talking chicken. And yet to an eager mind, absorbing a great story in every way, and lapping up every word, it's all unanticipated. It's all fresh, not frozen.

Somewhere in your pursuit of being grown up, did you stop absorbing and start anticipating? At some point in your spiritual journey, did you begin leaving words and events and experiences on the table of life and stop paying attention? And somewhere along the path, did you create some philosophical frameworks or little mental boxes to stuff all of life in because you anticipated it all, meaning that you brushed aside the stuff that didn't fit in your boxes?

Do you anticipate instead of participate in life?

Do you ever ask God a question and get an answer you didn't expect? What do you do with God's response when it doesn't fit your spiritual protocol?

God's like that, you know. God thinks of life in ways we don't, ways and thoughts that are greater and higher than ours.

So the next time you ask God a question, be prepared for anything, open to listening to life and making a life, not just a living.

Participate, don't anticipate, and ask God to hold your hand.

Listen to Your Life

1. How would God get a story through to you that doesn't fit your mental models?

2. If you're paid to provide leadership at work or answers on the job, how do you react when something occurs that you didn't anticipate?

3. What is the most honest, transparent, human response you can give when that happens?

Strategy 10: Ask to "Do It Again"
as Often as Possible

While our family was at a theme park, our younger daughter wanted to ride this really fast roller coaster, but her friend didn't want to. So our daughter said, "Daddy, will you ride with me?"

Of course, I said, "Yes!" It's a pretty big deal when your middle-school-aged daughter asks you to do anything with her in public. We waited in line together, talking about everything and nothing in particular; just enjoying spending time together. Our turn came to get on the roller coaster and we excitedly got on. I asked her, "Do you scream?" She said, "Yes" and I said, "Me, too."

When the ride was over and as we got off, she looked at me and said those wonderful words, "Daddy, can we do it again?" I remembered all those times she said that as a toddler when we played together. And you know what I said, don't you? "Of course we can, sweetheart!"

What was the last wonderful experience you had that you wanted to repeat? And like a child, just wanted to say, "Do it again, Daddy. Do it again!"? Moments like those are so precious that they bear repeating, don't they? If only you could...

...and in some ways, you can. I mean, what does it hurt to ask?

Especially when you listen to life like a child, and take the hand of God, your heavenly Daddy, who wants to ride with you through all of your life experiences, and can't wait to hear you say, "Can we do it again?" God truly receives pleasure from your pleasure and wants you to enjoy the best life has to offer.

So invite God to join you for the ride of your life and thrill God's heart as you reach up, take God's hand, listen to life like a child, and make a life, not just a living.

Listen to Your Life

1. What was your most recent thrilling experience?

2. Why would you want to "do it again?"

3. Have you asked God if you can? And invited God to join in on the fun? If not, take a moment and do so right now.

Strategy 11: Have Casual Conversations with God

A mother who listens to life through our newspaper column told me a story about her daughter. When the daughter was about two years old, the mother heard her one night in her bedroom, talking. So the mother went in the daughter's bedroom and discovered her standing up on her bed.

"What are you doing?" the mother asked.

The daughter said, "God told me to just stand."

The mother said, "Huh? God told you to just stand?"

"Yep," said the daughter, "God told me to just stand" and she was acting as if it was the most natural thing in the world for her to have a conversation with God and for God to say, "Just stand."

I wonder if in your mature adult sophistication, you forgot how to have a casual conversation with God and just do whatever God tells you to do? Like "just stand?" Do you have that kind of child-like faith that allows you to just obey a word from God?

That's a real challenge today, isn't it? You might want an independent counsel to study the findings of this word from God, from whence it came, if it actually was said, if so in what tone of voice, are the voice prints verifiably God's…you know, kind of a spiritual SSI (Spiritual Scene Investigation).

Man, it's a real challenge to just drop the suspicious mind

barriers and open up your spirit to a casual conversation with God, isn't it?

But isn't that what listening to life today for what God has to say and making a life, not just a living is all about? Being child-like?

Reach out and let God take your hand and "just stand" today, okay?

Listen to Your Life

1. Do you have a quiet place, away from everything and everyone that you can "just drop the suspicious mind barriers and open up your spirit to a casual conversation with God?" If not, discover one. Timing is important, too, because your place might be quiet for just an hour in the morning or after 5 p.m.

2. Go to that quiet place at the appointed time. (Shut the door if there's one.) Take three deep breaths, close your eyes, and say out loud, "Well, God, what do you want to talk about?"

3. Listen.

Strategy 12: Check on the People You Love

I heard from a friend who listens to life with us through our web site at www.listentolife.org about something she learned from a child. A three-year-old little girl loved her grandmother very much. She called her grandmother, Mimi.

Well, Mimi became very sick and eventually died. The little girl couldn't quite understand what had happened to her Mimi. So her parents took her to see Mimi's remains at the funeral home.

The little girl stared at her Mimi in the casket for several minutes, taking it all in, as her father held her. Then she reached down and touched Mimi's hand. Startled, she asked her dad, "What's wrong with Mimi? She's frozen!"

"Mimi is in heaven now. This is just what's left behind," her dad said.

The little girl stared for a moment, lost in her own thoughts, then ordered her dad, "Well, get God on the phone. I want to see how Mimi is."

(I never did find out how her father responded to that one!)

When you love someone, you care about her well-being. You want to know what's going on with him. Even when he leaves here to be with God. Even when her remains feel frozen.

As an adult, you know that not even today's advanced technology can get a call into heaven (conventionally speaking, of course). And you know the day is coming when you won't be able to see how your loved one is.

So why do you delay calling, or writing, or emailing, or something/anything that approximates holding that person's hand?

I know, we're all busy, but doing what—making a life or just a living?

Listen to Your Life

1. Whose hand would you hold right now if you could?

2. If that person is living, dog-ear this page, put down this book, and go make the call or send the email.

3. If that person is living somewhere else eternally, dog-ear this page, put down this book and pray, thanking God for the most excellent memories that flood your mind in that minute, or, write a letter to that person about those memories and get it to her/his closest living relative.

Strategy 13: Hold the Right Hand—God's

Do you remember when you were a child how excited you were getting ready for Santa Claus? You made your wish list of toys and treasures and impatiently waited until the night that lasts longer than any other night—Christmas Eve.

When she was a preschooler, our daughter anticipated the longest night of the year and dictated her Christmas wish list to her mother. You know the drill—the grandparents, uncles and aunts, and other family members want "a list" to buy from so they can get the best gifts.

One evening shortly after making her list, she and I knelt by her bed to pray. She hesitated for a moment, and then said, "Daddy, I want to pray to Santa Claus."

I was a little surprised by her remark. So I asked, "Why?"

And she said, "Because you won't let me ask God for toys so I want to ask Santa Claus."

It's so easy to stay right there—praying to Santa Claus—in your spiritual journey, isn't it? Of course, the older you get, the more expensive your toys. And maybe you don't just pray for toys. Maybe you pray for "good things" and even for other people. But your attitude in your spiritual journey is still that of regarding God like Santa Claus—"If I'm a good little boy/girl, I'll get what I want."

As you focus more and more of your energy on listening to life and making a life, not just a living, you discover that your "wants" become less important and God's "wants" more important. Soon, you realize that God provides all of your needs, knows your wants and provides many of those as well. So you listen to life and make a life, and your living becomes more profitable, too.

When you reach up for a hand in your journey, make sure you get the right one—God's.

Listen to Your Life

1. Make a prayer journal. It doesn't have to be anything fancy, just a few sheets of notebook paper will do. The form isn't important. The function is.

2. Write down in your prayer journal what you pray about, pray for; even write it down as you pray. Just follow the paths your mind walks.

3. About once a week, review where your heart goes in your prayers. Do you regard God as Santa Claus or God? Where does your heart-path of prayer need redirecting?

"Be Good"
Listen to Life with Your Hands

I t's really pretty simple, isn't it?

Treat others the way you want them to treat you.

The Golden Rule we call it.

You know it. You've heard it all your life, since you were a child.

So what happened?

When did you ditch the Golden Rule and pick up the Iron Rule—"Do unto others before they can do it to you"?

I'll bet you don't even remember. That's because it happens slowly at first, doesn't it? Not with a gush, but a gurgle. You start to look out for numero uno. After all, if you don't protect your own interests, who will? You keep your hands to yourself, and all the good gifts you can hold.

You're a sophisticated, mature adult now.

But you forget how to be good.

Or, is it really a matter of memory? Could it be a matter of means—and you choose the ends?

I don't know what it is other than to say it's a common mile marker of our human journey. And some of us never travel past that marker.

But we can. That's right, you can.

If you choose to treat others like you want them to treat you.

Not sure you remember how to be good?

Then here are nine strategies and stories about children to coach you to listen to life like a child and make a life by listening to life with your hands.

Strategy 1: Return Kind Acts

I traveled out of town to listen to life with some folks. It was time to eat and I was ready so I pulled into a restaurant.

As I went to the men's room, a little boy, about eight or nine years old went in ahead of me. He also made it to the sink ahead of me.

So as I stood there waiting for him to finish washing his hands, I rolled off some paper towels from the dispenser for him to use. You know, I was just trying to do something nice for him. "There you go, buddy," I said as he finished at the sink. And I went on over and started washing my hands.

As I washed my hands, the little fellow dried his off, and started rolling off paper towels from the dispenser for me to use. "There you go, sir," he said, smiled and walked out the door.

Now who would have thought it—a little guy returning a favor? I guess someone had taught him to return all kind acts.

What about you? Are you like this boy? When someone does something nice for you, do you return the favor?

It takes a little time, creativity, and sensitivity, doesn't it? Of course when you return a kind act, you're not restricted to return it just to the person who blessed you. You can be open to other opportunities with different people. For instance, let's say your car stalls out. A man jumps out of his SUV and helps you push your car into a parking lot. Odds are you won't get his name and won't be around when his SUV stalls. However, you invariably will be around someone else with a stalled vehicle. There's your opportunity to return the kind act—jump out and help push.

Now can you imagine the contagious chain of events that you'll infect others with as you return the favors you receive? Such a virus of kindness can infect neighborhoods, communities, cities, states, nations, even the world! And it all can start because of a little guy in a men's room, rolling off some paper towels.

Listen to life with your hands, and be good!

Listen to Your Life

1. Recall the last kind act someone did for you. What was it? Who did it? How did you feel when that person was kind to you?

2. Have you returned that kind act? If so, how? If not, why?

3. Ask God right now to present you with an opportunity today to return that kind act. Listen to your life very carefully today for your chance.

Strategy 2: Call God

A friend who listens to life with us through our newspaper column really loves his four-year-old grandson, Jake. Jake really enjoys life, learning about life and what it means to follow the rules of life.

Part of following the rules for Jake has been learning to dial 9-1-1 in case of an emergency. Recently, Jake dialed 9-1-1 and the call went something like this:

"9-1-1 Dispatcher. How can I help you?"

"Hi! My name is Jake and I need some help."

"Well, what's the problem, Jake?"

"I lost the remote control for the TV."

"Well, Jake, just get your mom or dad to help you find it."

"No, you don't understand. My dad will get really mad if I can't find it so I can't tell him or my mom."

Well, about that time Jake's mom walks up, takes the phone, and reassures the dispatcher that "Jake's dad will be just fine" and they'll find the remote. (I wonder what happened to Jake after his mom hung up the phone, don't you? Jake's dad may be fine, but what about Jake?!)

I guess we all have different kinds of emergencies, don't we? Your emergency might be different than mine, and mine is certainly different from someone else's. Regardless of the circumstances, you define your emergencies.

And when you're in the midst of an emergency, you look

for help. Jake dialed 9-1-1. He couldn't tell his mom and didn't dare tell his dad. So he turned to an obvious source of help, at least for a four-year-old.

What is your obvious source of help when you're distressed, worried, or have lost something important? A strategic part of listening to life and making a life, not just a living is knowing who to call in an emergency.

Listen to life with your hands and speed dial God.

Listen to Your Life

1. What is an emergency to you? Define what life situation constitutes your emergency.

2. How do you typically react to an emergency—worry, anger, depression, call God? Honestly reflect on your usual response.

3. Is that your best choice for a response? What is your preferred response? How will you respond next time to an emergency?

Strategy 3: Drop the Blame Game

A three-year-old girl lost her way. That is, she forgot how to behave properly or, if she remembered, she wasn't doing it. So her mother corrected her behavior, saying, "Now sweetheart, let's remember your manners."

And the little girl replied, "But Mommy, God forgot to give me my manners."

That's our first reaction, isn't it? When we're caught with our hand in life's cookie jar, I guess we're all looking for someone to blame, aren't we? I mean it can't be our fault, can it? The blame belongs with someone else. And God's so easy to blame. God doesn't talk back or act defensive.

But what is it that drives us to blame? Why can't we just accept the fact that we're not being good, that our hand is in the cookie jar and we're caught like the proverbial rat in a trap? We just don't want to take responsibility for our actions, do we?

You know what's really remarkable is that like this three-year-old, you can blame God for your misbehavior all you want, and God still loves you. In fact, God is present with you no matter what you do wrong and helps you find the way out of it—if you move beyond the blame game and take personal responsibility.

How do you do that? It's really quite simple:

1. Acknowledge your inappropriate behavior to those primarily concerned, including yourself.

2.   Apologize to whoever is involved, including anyone you blamed.

3.   Make amends with them.

God's got great manners to allow you a second chance to get it right, even when you blame God.

Wherever you are in your life and whatever you've done, just remember God loves you regardless of your manners. God will give you some new manners…just hold out your hands and ask for some more as you listen to life and make a life, not just a living.

Listen to Your Life

1.   Who did you last blame for your mistake? What was the mistake and why that person?

2.   What do you plan to do about the mistake and the ensuing blame?

3.   Re-read the simple, three-step process above and follow it.

Strategy 4: Share

My wife decided we needed some of those outdoor chairs that you can fold up, put in a sack, and carry across your shoulder. So we went to the store and bought the last two they had.

Not too long after that, we went to an outdoor family event. A band played dance music and there were amusements for the children and of course, lots to eat and drink. There were three of us in our family that went that night and we took the new chairs. And that meant one of us had to stand—three people, two chairs.

Well, being the "nice guy" that I am, I told my wife and daughter to have the chairs and that I would stand. After standing for just a few minutes, a man that I didn't know comes over and tells me that he has an extra chair if I'd like to use it. Evidently he watched as we unfolded our chairs and saw I didn't have one. He promised me that he didn't need it and I went over, got the chair, and sat down.

A month later, we went to a similar outdoor event. Only this time, we had gone to a department store and bought a couple of more chairs. So we had four chairs, but as it was previously, there were only three of our family members present.

So I put three chairs in the trunk of my car and away we went. Well, when we got to the event, I took the three chairs out of the trunk. And our younger daughter looked at me and said, "Daddy, where's the other chair?"

"I didn't bring it with us, honey," I said. "There are only three of us tonight."

"But, Daddy," she said, "We could have let someone use the extra chair like that nice man did for you last time."

Do you want to "be good?" Then listen to life and make a life with your hands...and share.

Listen to Your Life

1. Recall a time when someone unexpectedly went out of their way to help you.

2. What was your reaction?

3. Plan for the next time you can unexpectedly help someone. Prepare to share.

Strategy 5: Laugh

A mother invited some friends over for dinner. They were all seated at the table, ready to eat. The piping hot food steamed on the table. The glasses were filled with beverages. Every place was set perfectly. She was pleased with her table!

So she turned to her six-year old daughter and said, "Would you like to say the blessing?"

"I wouldn't know what to say," the little girl told her mother.

"Just say what you hear me say," the mother said.

So the daughter bowed her head, folded her hands, and said, "O God, why on earth did I invite all these people to dinner?"

I guess the good news is that we did the same thing to our parents and not only did we live to laugh about it later, our parents came out of it okay, too. And probably the best news of all is that God, who hears these interesting prayers and other unexpected words from our mouths, claps divine hands and laughs about it, and comes out of it all just fine.

Well, if God laughs, what about you? When was the last time you threw your head back and just roared with laughter?

There are so many uptight people in the world, so many folks who take everything so seriously and make a federal case out of the tiniest detail—seen Court TV?—you don't have to be one of them. Laughter really is the best medicine. It does a body good…and your heart, too.

Frankly, I am my own best material. I laugh at myself every day for something, whether it's a bone-head stunt or something I say or forget to do. Just looking in the mirror every morning gets me laughing! ("Where did all my hair go? Oh, there it is on my shoulders…")

Clap your hands. Slap your thighs. Flap your gums and laugh. Like a child.

Now there…isn't that better?

Listen to Your Life

1. What do you think the mother's face looked like after her daughter prayed?

2. How do you think "all these people" reacted to the prayer?

3. Imagine the table conversation for the next five minutes as they passed the roast beef and mashed potatoes, green beans and carrots. Who said what?

Strategy 6: Care

Some days you just feel like dancing, don't you? I mean life is so good and sweet and everything's goin' your way. Some days you just have to dance.

One day, when our older daughter was in elementary school, she just had to dance. She danced barefooted through our kitchen while my wife fixed dinner.

My wife told our daughter repeatedly, "Please don't dance in the kitchen." But sometimes little girls just can't help themselves. They just have to dance.

My wife set the table and our daughter's milk glass was already on the table. As she danced, she pirouetted too closely to the dinner table, knocked her milk glass to the floor, spilling milk everywhere and, of course, the glass broke into a thousand, tiny, sharp pieces.

What would be your first response to that?

"I told you to stop dancing!"

"You never listen to me!"

"You're gonna have to clean that up!"

But there was none of that this time. My wife moved quickly to our daughter's side and asked, "Are you OK? Are you cut anywhere?" as she picked her up and moved safely away from the broken glass.

The first reaction has more to do with the need to be right. My wife's reaction is all about care.

It's more important to use your hands to care than to prove you're right.

God moves to your side like my wife when you've broken something in your life. When you dance and something goes wrong, God comes to care for you.

And God wants you to be divine hands that care. So listen to life with your hands, be good, and give care instead of proving you're right.

Listen to Your Life

1. What would have been your first reaction to our daughter's accident? (Be honest now...yea, mine too.)

2. Why do you work so hard to prove you're right?

3. Today, find one opportunity to care instead of proving you're right, and seize it. Watch the reactions of the people involved. Plan to do it again tomorrow.

Strategy 7: Ask for Forgiveness

A mother who listens to life through our web site at www.listentolife.org emailed me a story about how one Wednesday evening, she, along with her husband and two boys were walking down the hallway of their church facility. Once again, she and her husband were talking with their sons about where they were and that God expected them to "be good" in God's house.

Their four-year-old son looked up at his daddy and huge tears began to stream down his face. "What's wrong, son?" the father asked.

And the little boy said, "I want to be good Daddy, but I just can't sometimes."

Can you relate to that little boy—"I want to be good, but I just can't sometimes?" I know I can. In fact, sometimes it seems that the harder I try to be good, the more I do things that aren't good.

Now why is that? Maybe instead of trying to be good, I already know I'm not always good. And so instead of trying to be good, I try not to be bad. And when I'm focused on the bad, not the good, that's what I do—the bad. Make sense?

Well, it's okay either way, because God knows you can't be good all the time. That sometimes the harder you try to be good, the more you're not. And so God created this wonderful ability to make you good even when you're not—forgiveness.

The first step to receiving forgiveness is to do what this little boy did with tear-filled eyes: realize and admit that you're not always good. Even though you try to be good, sometimes you're not. Confessing that to God releases the floodgates of forgiveness from the eternal streams of heaven.

Ask God for forgiveness today when you can't be good as you listen to life and make a life, not just a living.

Listen to Your Life

1. Remember the last occasion in which you knew what the right thing to do was, but you didn't do it.

2. Why did you choose not to be good? Any idea?

3. Admit to God that you could have chosen better and didn't. Ask God to forgive you and help you listen to your life and make a better decision next time.

Strategy 8: Ask for Help

Help comes in all kinds of ways, doesn't it?

A police officer was at an elementary school, taking a vandalism report. As the officer filled out the paper work, a little girl, probably a kindergartner, walked over and just stood there, looking up at him.

"Can I help you?" the officer asked.

"Are you a police officer?" the little girl said.

"Yes, I am," the officer said.

"My mommy said that if I ever needed any help that I should ask a police officer. Is that right?" she said.

"Yes," said the officer, "that's right."

"Well then," she said as she stuck out her foot, "would you please tie my shoe?"

We all need some help at some time in our lives, don't we? And sometimes the help someone else needs may seem pretty easy to you—like tying a shoe—but it sure is important to them. I'm sure that little girl didn't want to fall and hurt herself while playing. Skinned knees hurt.

You may think at times in your spiritual journey that your request for help may seem too small to God. I mean, what with starvation, HIV/AIDS, and war to contend with, God probably just doesn't have time to fool with your petty predicament.

Nothing could be further from the truth! Sure, God's concerned with the "big issues" of life, but God's also intimately involved in your life, ready to help with all of them from the "smallest" to the "largest." (But they all seem large when the problem is yours, don't they?)

An integral part of learning to listen to life and make a life, not just a living is learning to ask for help. God is ready and listening for you.

Listen to Your Life

1. How can you tell when you would like some help?

2. What keeps you from asking God for help?

3. The next time you sense you would like some help, but are hesitant to ask, say to yourself, "God is ready and listening for me." Then ask for help.

Strategy 9: Run TO, not FROM God

My wife tells the story from her childhood of decorating the Christmas tree along with the rest of her family one Christmas Eve. All of a sudden, there comes a knock on the door. One of her five older sisters answers the door, and says, "Well, Santa Claus! Come on in! Are you here to see my little sister?"

Like she's shot out of a cannon, my wife takes off running for her bedroom, scared to death that Santa Claus has come on Christmas Eve and she's not ready for him. Her mind runs through a laundry list of ways she's not prepared:

- She's not laid out his milk and cookies.
- She's not said her bedtime prayers.
- She's not in bed, asleep.
- She's not going to get any toys!

Though they coaxed her in every known way, she never did come out of her bedroom to see Santa. She ran from, not to, the jolly ole elf.

Like my wife was with Santa, sometimes your first reaction to God showing up in your life is what you haven't done. You think you must be perfect for God to give you any presents. And yet you know you can't be perfect so you run away from God.

And yet, as you've read in this section, "be good" isn't God's way of demanding perfection from you. Rather, it is God's way of drawing you into a closer relationship, knowing that the only way you can truly be good is in a personal, intimate relationship with God. Your goodness doesn't depend on your perfection. Your goodness emerges from God's perfection and your connection with it.

Run TO, not FROM God. Run to God and:

- become good, not perfect;
- listen to life like a child, and;
- make a life, not just a living.

Listen to Your Life

1. Relive the last time you ran from God. What did you do that wasn't perfect?

2. When you tired of running from God, what did you do then?

3. Have you come back, run to God yet? If not, what's holding you back?

"Look Both Ways"
Listen to Life with Your Attitude

You see what you're looking for.

You hear what you're listening for.

You are what you see and hear.

And what's the underlying, motivating power behind your choosing what to see and hear, i.e., what you are?

Attitude.

Think about it for a minute. It's a rainy day. And it's a Monday. Now what's your typical attitude toward such a day?

What if your area is experiencing a drought? Now what's your attitude?

But what if the drought has made the ground hard and the rain is falling so forcefully that it's simply sheeting off, no real chance for the ground to absorb it. What's your attitude now?

Did your perception of the rain change with each new slice of information?

Now, what would a child see on such a rainy day?

- Mud puddles to play in.
- Rivers to stand in and watch the water splash up your legs.
- Boat races with leaves and twigs.
- Bathwater for birds.

- "Can I go fishing?"
- God watering the flowers and grass and trees.

You see what you're looking for.

You hear what you're listening for.

You are what you see and hear.

Attitude. Does yours need adjusting? Then here are twelve strategies and stories about children to coach you to listen to life like a child by looking both ways and growing a better attitude.

Strategy 1: Expect God

I like music of all types. Frankly, I'm more interested in good lyrics than I am anything else. And yet, when I find a song that's got great lyrics and music, I just want to listen to it over and over.

Buddy Jewell's song, *Help Pour Out the Rain (Lacey's Song)* is just such a song. I heard him interviewed recently and he said he got the inspiration for the song while taking his four-year-old daughter to preschool. She said to him, just out of the blue, "Daddy, I don't want to go to heaven."

And he said, "Well, you might want to reconsider that, honey. I hear they don't have air-conditioning in the other place."

She thought for a minute, then said, "Well, I don't want to go right now, but when I go, can I help pour out the rain?"

Buddy's song wrote itself right out of that life experience with his preschool daughter. He listened to life like a child through his daughter.

These kinds of events don't happen just to Buddy Jewell. Sure, he took the experience and turned it into a hit song. In your spiritual journey, you have similar encounters if you listen to life with an open, searching attitude. How does that work?

Such an attitude grows in the fertile soil of an expectant outlook on life. You expect God to share unconditional love with you somehow, sometime, in some way that day. You participate fully in the experiences of that day. Sometimes your preschooler asks about heaven. Other times, she pitches a fit. God speaks to you through both, if you're listening to your life and earnestly expecting to make a life, not just seeing yourself as moved around by unseen forces in life that care nothing about you. You openly search for God in all of life.

So look both ways as you live each day. Look in, under, around, and through every event for God. And know that as you listen to your life and seek to make a life, not just a living, God will give you your heartsong.

Listen to Your Life

1. What would be your reaction if your daughter or grand-daughter said, "I don't want to go to heaven?"

2. How did Buddy Jewell "look both ways" in responding to his daughter's comment?

3. Name three ways you can "look both ways" in listening to your life and opening up an expectant, searching attitude toward God.

Strategy 2: Look Beyond the Usual

A five-year-old little boy was at the beach with his family. He's an inquisitive child, purely honest as he listens to life, and doesn't hesitate to comment on what he hears.

Well, while he's at the beach with his family, he saw an African-American little boy about his age. The boy's mother, who is Caucasian, was with him. The first little boy, who's also Caucasian, stared at the mother and child. Being so curious, he asked the mother, "Is that your little boy?"

And the mother replied, "Yes, he's my little boy."

"Well," he said, "he doesn't look like you."

About this time, his mother walked up, heard the conversation, and held her breath, praying her son didn't offend the woman and her son.

The woman said, "What do you mean?"

And the curious little boy replied, "Well, he has curly hair and you have straight hair."

And what did you think he'd say?

I'll bet you thought he would comment on the difference in the color of their skin. And why not? Wouldn't you?

Bigots aren't born.

We learn prejudice.

God's love is actually what's born within us.

This little guy's open search for God in his life caused him to look beyond the obvious that you and I see into something else, something not conflicted, but simply loving. He looked both ways, not just down the path of "usual."

With love in your heart, listen to life today and make a life, not just a living as you look both ways, i.e., the "usual" and the "unusual."

Listen to Your Life

1. What do you notice first about people?

2. How quickly do you make judgments about them based on appearance?

3. Why do you do that? What attitudes do you have that support it? Do you want to change those attitudes?

Strategy 3: Look Both Ways for Abundance

All of the children were lined up in the cafeteria of a religious school, waiting to get their lunch. They seemed to be waiting patiently, but you could tell they were hungry.

At the head of the table was this humongous pile of apples. I mean you've never seen so many apples on one table and they were all so beautiful and red. I guess because they looked so delicious, the principal had attached to the table a note: "Take only one apple. God is watching you."

Moving through the line, to the other end of the same table, was another humongous pile, only this time of chocolate chip cookies. I mean you've never seen so many chocolate chip cookies on one table and they were still warm and smelled so good. I guess because they looked so delicious, one of the children had attached to the table this note: "Take all you want. God is watching the apples."

So which God is your God—the God of the apples or the God of the chocolate chip cookies?

You know it's so easy as you journey through life to convince yourself that there's not enough to go around. That there's a limited amount of apples (or whatever) and that you'd better get yours and warn off everyone else, invoking God's watchful, cosmic eye. Instead, change your attitude to one of abundance, realizing that apples are growing somewhere daily and that when those are gone, there will be some more because that's what apples do—God made them to grow.

So look both ways in your journey through life and discover that there really is enough to go around...and God is watching the supply of everything to insure there is!

Listen to Your Life

1. So which God is your God—a God of scarcity or the God of abundance?

2. What fear drives you to look just one way, toward scarcity?

3. Listen to your thoughts and conversations today and try to look toward abundance—the knowledge that God provides everything we need. Say words that promote abundance. Think abundant thoughts. Watch your attitude transform.

Strategy 4: Look for Something Big

O ur older daughter and I were going home one evening and we passed by a Christmas tree sales yard. There were lots and lots of trees for sale when all of a sudden she said, "None of those trees look very big."

"No, they don't look big on the lot," I said. "That's because the lot is wide-open, no ceiling or walls. But when you get those trees home, they get bigger."

"But they're cut down. How do they get bigger?" she asked.

"They get bigger to your eyes once they're at home because you bring them inside," I said.

You know, a lot of things get bigger to your eyes once they're at home, inside. Especially to our children's eyes. We spend so much time and money buying them plastic toys or designer clothes or electronic dolls, all of which get smaller after a few days at home.

We forget the things that get bigger in their eyes once they're at home, inside.

Things like "I love you!" for no reason at all.

A hug and kiss for something they did well.

"How was your day?" when they look a little down.

So what are you bringing inside your home?

If you're just making a living, about all you bring inside are those plastic toys, designer clothes, or electronic dolls along with a huge dose of stress, some dissatisfaction, and an uneasy, peace-less feeling.

If you make a living, but focus your primary spiritual energy on making a life then you bring inside love and laughter, hugs and happiness, peace and purpose.

As you journey through life today, look for something big; bigger than just making a living. Listen to your life and make a life!

Listen to Your Life

1. If you asked some children, "What's big to you?" what do you think they would say?

2. If you want to listen to life like a child, how does your attitude and accompanying behaviors need to change about what's big?

3. What is one attitude that you can start changing today about what's big?

Strategy 5: Look for It to Happen to You

Have you ever noticed how something can happen to someone else and it's not a big deal? But when it happens to you, all of a sudden it transforms into something huge?

Take surgery for instance. Someone else has "minor surgery." Never mind if it's quadruple heart by-pass surgery. "They do that every day now," you say. But when it's your turn to have surgery, something like a hernia repaired, then your surgery is "major."

Here's a case in point: Four-year-old Zachary came running out of the bathroom. "Mommy! Mommy!" he screamed. "I dropped my toothbrush in the toilet." So Mommy fished it out and threw it in the garbage.

Zachary stood there thinking for a moment, then ran to his mother's bathroom and came out with her toothbrush. He held it up and said with a charming little smile, "We better throw this one out too then, 'cause it fell in the toilet last week."

See what I mean? When it's your toothbrush in the toilet, it's a different story altogether.

Why? I don't know. I guess because we're self-consuming.

But what if…you act as if someone else's toothbrush is your own?

And you imagine that someone else's surgery is your own?

How would your attitude toward making a life change?
Would you be looking both ways then?

When you hear about some event in another person's life, imagine it is happening to you. Go to that friend or family member and empathize, not just sympathize. Share with them and care for them as you would want someone to do for you.

When you do, you listen to life and make a life, not just a living!

Listen to Your Life

1. Who do you know that finds him or herself in a situation that is "major?"

2. How would you feel and what would you think if it were you in that situation?

3. Go to that person. Share and care today.

Strategy 6: Look Both Ways
for the "Other Meaning"

A mother who listens to life with us through www.listentolife.org sent me an email about how much her youngest son wanted a Nerf Gun. Finally she gave in and bought him one.

He was so proud of his new toy. He begged her, "Mom, can I please carry my new toy to school tomorrow?" She said, "No son, you are not allowed to carry toys to school, especially a gun."

Well, he continued asking all evening. So finally his mother said, "Son, let's sleep on it and I will let you know in the morning." And it worked! He was quiet the rest of the evening.

The next morning she woke him up and said that it was time to get ready for school. The little fellow jumped up quickly, lifted his pillow and said, "Mom, I slept on my Nerf Gun all night just like you said. Can I please carry it to school today and show my friends?"

The mother said one thing and understood what she meant.

The little boy heard another thing and understood something quite different.

God knows that you don't always understand what to do with life's gifts. Sometimes God says one thing and you hear something else. Other times God means something and you understand something quite different.

So what do you do?

You listen to life with the assurance that God knows you won't understand the divine direction every time. That sometimes you sleep on something, hoping against hope that God has a change of mind. Other times, you go on and do what you desire anyway, without asking God.

Now with that assurance tucked snuggly in your heart, look both ways in your life's journey for the "other meaning." Your tendency is to make God "fit" into your preferred way of doing life. Resist that temptation. Look for what else God could mean, might intend for you to do in the situation. Consider the other possibilities for divine meaning.

Then after you discover the "other meaning," sleep on it, and take it into life with you the next morning as you listen to life and make a life.

Listen to Your Life

1. Recall an experience in which you thought someone—your boss, spouse, God—meant one thing by a statement, but actually intended something entirely different, something you had not even considered.

2. What happened for you once you realized what that person really meant? How did you feel? What did you think?

3. Consider carefully what God whispers in your heart's ear today. Play a mental game with yourself and think about God's words from every possible angle, considering all semantic variables. When you discover one that causes you to feel peaceful, stay with that one.

Strategy 7: Look for "Not Yet's"

It was a big day around our home. Our younger daughter celebrated her 13th birthday. Yes, I know, it was hard for me to believe, as well, that I could be old enough for my "baby girl" to turn 13, but nonetheless, she did and I obviously am.

I had the privilege of driving her to school that morning. She's not very talkative in the mornings on the way to school normally, but this morning she was a little brighter eyed. A few nights earlier she had her first "boy-girl" birthday party. She was wearing her new shoes and a special outfit—all birthday presents. She had every reason to be a little brighter eyed.

So I asked her, "Do you feel any different now that you're a teenager?" And she said, "Not yet!"

Don't you just love that response—"Not yet!" She meant, "I know it's coming and I can't wait for it to get here, but not yet!"

Do you anticipate your participation in life with that kind of wonderful attitude? That today holds something special and it's coming, but not here yet?

It's so easy to you to choose to form your attitude in reaction to what's going on around you rather than choosing your attitude and letting it form your reaction to the world. For instance, think about the weather—the most discussed topic anywhere and the one you can do the least about. Do you react to the weather—whether it's a sunny Friday or rainy Monday? Or, do you choose your attitude proactively—knowing that something good is coming even though it may "not yet" be here?

Develop a "not-yet" attitude as an integral part of your listening to life and making a life, not just a living. Cultivate your heart desire to look forward to today's "not yet's." Life is what you make of it. Choosing a "not-yet" perspective as you participate in today's events helps you lean into the goodness of life, qualities like kindness and love, peace and joy. And as you lean, these qualities come to you.

Regardless of what today brings you, know that something wonderful is on its way, it's just "not yet" here!

Listen to Your Life

1. Honestly evaluate how much circumstances beyond your control, e.g., the weather, affect your attitude toward life. On a scale of 1 to 10, with 1 being no affect and 10 being total affect, where would you rank yourself?

2. If you could choose any attitude for yourself, what would it be?

3. Having named that attitude, choose it—because you can. Declare it your "new attitude." Write it on a note card and tape it to your make-up or shaving mirror, put it on the dash of your vehicle, or somewhere you can see it daily. Repeat your "new attitude" constantly, saying, "My attitude is…"

Strategy 8: Look Both Ways for "Why?"

Do you just take things for granted as the way they have been, are, and always will be?

Children have a natural curiosity that drives them to ask "Why?" about everything. They want to understand. In fact, every three-year-old I've ever been around constantly asked, "Why?" And regardless of how many wonderful answers you produced, the common response was, "Why?"

For example, a nursery school teacher was delivering a van full of children home one day when a fire truck zoomed past. Sitting in the front seat of the fire truck was a Dalmatian dog. One of the children asked, "Why does the Dalmatian dog ride on the fire truck?"

"They use him to keep crowds back," said one child.

"No," said another, "he's just for good luck."

A third child brought the argument to a close. "They use the dogs," she said firmly, "to find the fire hydrants."

I guess we just take it for granted that Dalmatians ride on fire trucks without asking, "Why?" What else do you take for granted, not examining the cause behind it, or the purpose of doing it a certain way?

Do you just let tradition box you in? Or, do you ask, "Why?"

If you want to listen to life like a child, you simply must develop again an attitude of "Why?" I know how easy it is to allow the inertia of tradition, the comfort of routine, and the familiarity of habit flood the life out of your natural curiosity. But if you want to make a life, not just a living, and enjoy life in all its rich textures and fullness of hues, you simply must develop more "Why?"

Why? Because by probing beneath the surface of everyday living, you preserve the fire in your belly to interact with the world, knowing that God is there already working, rather than worshipping the ashes of the ritual of an unexamined life.

Listen to Your Life

1. Find a three-year-old—borrow a friend's, go to a daycare, whatever it takes—and talk with the child. Or, just listen to their conversations, particularly with adults. Tune your spiritual ears to listen not only to the "Why?s" but the earnest spirit of wonderment behind the question.

2. Start looking at what you do daily—your routines like driving to work or getting ready in the mornings. Think about why you do what you do? Examine everything—why you shave the way you shave or brush your hair the way you do.

3. Try doing something different. Start shaving on the other side of your face. Brush your hair from the other side first. Drive a different route to work. Notice what happens to your spiritual curiosity as you do.

Strategy 9: Look for Honesty

Have you ever noticed how honest children are? Sometimes, brutally honest? They don't mean to say what they say exactly how they say it. They just ask honest questions and tell the truth as they see it with an innocence that you just can't argue with. They just can't help themselves, can they? But their innocent logic is flawless most of the time, isn't it?

Take for example, a little girl who was sitting at the kitchen counter, watching her mother do some cooking. All of a sudden, she noticed that her mother had several strands of white hair sticking out on her otherwise brunette head. So she looked at her mother and asked, "Why are some of your hairs white, Mama?" And her mother said, "Well, every time that you do something wrong and make me cry or unhappy, one of my hairs turns white."

The little girl thought about this for a minute and then said, "Mama, how come ALL of Grandma's hairs are white?"

Now that's honest!

Children make connections between life events pretty well, don't they? They don't cloud their minds and spirits with half-truths or half-lies. They just piece life together with an honest, open approach to what they observe.

So when did you lose that quality?

Probably when you got caught somewhere along life's path with your hand in the proverbial cookie jar, crumbs around your

Toll FREE 1-877-4DRJOEY

mouth, and managed to talk someone into another version of reality. Or, at least you thought you did.

To listen to life like a child you must be honest. First and foremost, you must be surgically honest with yourself—who you are, what you do well and enjoy, how you treat others, etc. Then be honest with others.

Being honest won't keep your hair from turning white, but it will keep you listening to life like a child and making a life, not just a living…honest!

Listen to Your Life

1. When are you most tempted to be dishonest?

2. When is it easiest for you to be honest?

3. What would happen if you were honest when you're most tempted? Not just to you, but your relationships with others?

Strategy 10: Look Around for Patience

I spent some time with a friend who was a new mother, i.e., a first-time mother whose baby was about a day old. She said, "Well, this baby is already teaching me a lot. Before he was born, I imagined all the things I needed to teach him. But then I realized even before he was born, that he was teaching me."

"What are you learning from him?" I said.

"Well, as you know, I thought he'd never get here. I've been ready to have him for weeks now," she said. "But I learned patience from him, that waiting is what we have to do sometimes whether we like it or not."

Isn't it great that God uses our children, even before they're born, to teach us? I don't know about you, but patience is one of those lessons I have to learn over and over again. Regardless of who the teacher is, even some surprising teachers at times, patience is one of those life lessons I struggle to learn. What about you?

"W-a-i-t" is a four letter word, isn't it? But what a marvelous way to listen to life! Think about all the ways you wait:

- Parents wait nine months for a baby to be born.
- You wait all your life to turn 13 years old, then 16, then 18, then 21, then retirement age.
- You wait at traffic lights, in traffic jams, behind slow traffic, and to merge with traffic.

Toll FREE 1-877-4DRJOEY

- You wait in the doctor's office, dentist's office, chiropractor's office, and pharmacy.

- You wait for a web page to download, email to arrive, and your friend to respond to your IM.

- You wait for a loved one to get well, prayers to be answered, and death to come.

You have so many opportunities to learn to listen to life like a child while waiting, growing more and more patient, right? Then use your wait wisely. Develop patience from a heart that's grateful God is patient with you.

Listen to Your Life

1. How patient are you?

2. What circumstances seem to short-circuit your patience quickest?

3. Knowing this, how can you best respond to these circumstances in a more patient manner? While you wait, grow that patient manner.

Strategy 11: Focus on Making a Life

A mother who listens to life with us told me the story of calling home one morning to check on her children. Her elementary school-aged daughter answered the phone. Before she said good-bye, the mother told the daughter, "Be nice to your brother today. You know, he didn't make the All-Star team and he may be kind of sad."

"Yea, I know, Mom," said the daughter, "but Mama, life's not about baseball."

"Okay," said the mother, "what's life about?"

"Well," the daughter said, "life's about...life!"

You know, that little girl is so right. How often in life do you focus on the things that go wrong—the team you didn't make, the promotion you didn't get, the vehicle you can't afford, the exotic trip you didn't take, the house you couldn't buy, the parent that died, the marriage that failed, the child who disappointed, and the list just goes on? All of these things that go wrong can become what your life is all about.

Of course, all of these events are a part of life. But they are just that—things that happen in life. They are not the sum total of who you are. They comprise a portion of your experiences. They do not constitute your being as a human.

But life really is about life. It's a mystery, a commingling of events both positive and negative—depending on your attitude—that are a part of you, but not all of you. You are more than your experiences. You are also how you choose to live after these experiences, because of these experiences, and in spite of these experiences.

You can't know exactly what today holds. But you do know who holds today as a gift—God. So let life be life as you listen to life like a child and make a life, not just a living.

Listen to Your Life

1. Look at the list of "wrong" things above. Which one jumps off the page at you?

2. How have you allowed that event to determine your attitude?

3. Do you want to continue to live with that determination? If not, what other attitude do you choose?

Strategy 12: Look Longer

Sometimes I feel like I'm just wasting my time. I try and try to do something and for whatever reason, it just won't work. Maybe I don't know what I'm doing. Or, the people I'm trying to do it with want to do anything but what I'm trying to do. And at other times, try as I will, I just can't do it.

Do you know what I'm talking about? If you do, maybe you can relate, like I can, with a little girl who had just finished her first week of school.

Her mother asked her, "So what do you think of your first week of school?"

"You don't want to know," she told her mother.

"Well, why not?" the mother said.

"Because you're not going to like what I say," the little girl said.

"Try me anyway," said the mother.

"Okay," she said to her mother. "I'm just wasting my time. I can't read, I can't write and they won't let me talk!"

Do you ever feel like you're just wasting your time? The next time you do, look around and take a little longer look, like from God's eternal perspective, at what you're doing. It may be that you can't do it right now, but will learn how sooner than you think.

The process of learning how to do something often takes time. And when you can't do something right away, it's very easy to feel like this first-grade girl—you're wasting time. That feeling is closely related to failure so in today's hurry-up-and-get-it-done culture, you're encouraged, in effect, not to take the time to learn how to do something, and not to admit your perceived inadequacy. The little girl felt like she was already supposed to know how to read and write when she didn't. What she knew how to do—talk—wasn't allowed. So she was wasting her time. Can you relate?

Lighten up on yourself. If you don't know how to do something, say so and pursue the resources for learning.

And most important of all—look longer, as in from God's eternal perspective. A little time spent learning is brief compared with forever. Redeem your time and keep learning.

Listen to Your Life

1. When did you last feel like you were wasting time?

2. Why did you choose to feel like you were wasting time?

3. How would you describe "forever?"

"Play Nice"
Listen to Life with Your Spirit

We have four blueberry bushes on our farm. The first year our family moved to the farm, the blueberry bushes were a reasonable size and produced so many delicious berries, we invited just about everyone we knew to come and pick some. The next year, the bushes grew some, not much, due to a drought. And there were a lot of berries, but maybe not as many as the year before. The third year on the farm, the drought ended and the bushes grew very tall, but didn't produce as many berries as the year before, and a lot less than the first year.

So I decided to discover why we had fewer and fewer berries each year. What I found out was this: blueberry bushes require pruning. If the bush isn't pruned, then "creepers" or immature branches develop. They drain the bush of vital nutrients that should be going to more mature, berry-producing branches. Pretty soon, the creepers take over, the mature portions atrophy, and you have very few if any berries. All because I didn't prune.

Now you might think, like I did, that since the bush is growing, there should be more berries. Not so. The pruning process, when done correctly, rids the bush of the creepers and allows the bush's strength—the mature branches—to flourish and produce. Pruning plays to the bush's best. Not pruning allows the weakness of the bush to bully the others.

Remembering how to play nice in life is like pruning. There are some ways to play that are better than others and some that are weaker.

Where does your play need pruning? Here are ten strategies and stories about children to coach you to listen to life like a child and grow your spirit in nice, strong ways.

Strategy 1: Let Others Know Who You Are

My brother and his wife had a little girl, Caroline. She's their second child. Their son, Joe, was two-and-a-half years old when Caroline was born.

Well, of course, she was beautiful from birth. I knew that as I traveled to see them. While there, I really enjoyed seeing my new niece and spending some time with Joe.

While we were in the hospital room, Joe wanted some water. So I walked him down to the nurses' station to get him a big cup with a straw like his mom's. As we walked back, I said to him, "Joe, you're Caroline's big brother."

"I Carowine's big brudder?" he asked.

"Yes, you are," I said, "just like I'm your Daddy's big brother."

"You Daddy's big brudder?" he said.

"Yes I am, just like you're Caroline's big brother," I told him.

Well, when we got back to the room, Joe wanted to get in the bed with his mother who was holding Caroline. So I picked him up, he crawled over to Caroline, and said with the sweetest little voice, "Carowine, I your big brudder."

Do you let other people know who you are? Not just your name, but more than that? It's pretty basic to shake hands with someone, grunt your name and a "Nice to meet you," without really letting them know who you are. Get to know someone by:

- Asking about where they live, where they work, etc.
- Making common points of connection with home town, work, etc.
- Establishing your relationship with the person, e.g., I usually say, "I'm your speaker today."

Letting people know who you are, not just your name, but your relationship with them, is an important first step to building intimacy. Too often, culture pushes you toward seeing people as commodities, "things" to use, "resources" to employ in the accomplishment of a task. If you are to lead in any environment, building intimacy which proves you are worthy of trust is your first step to success. To listen to life like a child, think of it as the first step to playing nice. After all, we're all children of God, right?

Listen to Your Life

1. Reflect on the last time you met someone. Recall how, if at all, you interacted with that person beyond, "Hello, (insert name here)."

2. The next time you meet someone, try just one of the suggestions above and see how the person responds.

3. Prepare a list of qualities you believe are important about you. Remember them so you can share some of them with the next person you meet.

Strategy 2: Use Your Special Powers

A friend who listens to life with us told me the story of her six-year-old son walking up to her one day and saying, "Mommy, God gave me special powers!"

"Oh really," she said. "What kind of special powers did God give you?"

And the little boy said, "I can talk to animals and they understand me."

Well, of course, the first thing the mother thought, "Oh! He's another Dr. Doolittle," but she said to him, "Really? Well, how do you know God gave you this special power?"

And he said, "Because I tell our dog, 'I love you,' and she licks my face."

You know, God gives us all a special power—the power of love. We can tell each other, "I love you" and give each other love back.

Can you imagine what a wonderful world this will be as more of us start using our special power of love? And defining power not as money, success, or military strength, but love?

The key to listening to your life like a child is for you to believe that you really do have this power, and that this power is really that special. You can be a part of creating this wonderful world where this special power of love rules...if you use your special powers God gave you.

The best characteristic about your special powers is that you

don't have to dress up like a freak in colorful tights, conceal-
ing your secret identity from your family, and travel differently.
(But then again, the Batmobile looks pretty cool, doesn't it?
And how about the view from Spiderman's perch?) You only
have to be yourself at home, at work, in the grocery store, at
the coffee shop, and everywhere else you go.   Those are the
places where you—yes, you—can use your special powers of
love.

The ways you can use your special powers are endless!
Your imagination is your only limit in finding ways to say "I
love you!" to people.

So tell someone "I love you!" as you listen to life like a child
today and enjoy making a life, not just a living.

Listen to Your Life

1. Write down three ways you can use your special powers
    with your family.

2.   Write down three ways you can use your special powers
    at work.

3. Write down three ways you can use your special powers at
    the grocery store.

Strategy 3: Play Nice Even When You Don't Want To

Did you hear about the Texas teacher who was helping one of her kindergarten students put on his cowboy boots? She pulled and he pushed, but the little boots wouldn't go on. Finally, after too much stress and strain, the boots were on.

She almost cried when the little boy said, "Teacher, they're on the wrong feet." She looked and sure enough, they were. She managed to keep her cool as together they worked to get the boots back on the right feet.

He then announced, "These aren't my boots." She bit her tongue rather than get right in his face and scream, "Why didn't you say so?" like she wanted to. And, once again she helped him pull the boots off his little feet.

They got the boots off and he said, "They're my brother's boots. My Mom made me wear 'em."

Now she didn't know if she should laugh or cry but she wrestled the boots on his feet again. "Now," she said, "where are your mittens?"

And he said, "I stuffed 'em in the toes of my boots."

Life is more challenging some days than others, isn't it? Some days, playing nice with others is so easy—a breeze, a piece of cake, no sweat. Other days, playing nice is an option distantly removed from your consciousness—you can barely remember how, but at the forefront of your memory is how to choke someone! You can relate with this teacher on those days, can't you?

Playing nice with others even when you don't want to is tough sometimes. The only way I've discovered to treat others the way I want to be treated, even when they're wearing out my "last nerve" is to have made the choice to play nice ahead of time, to decide in advance that I will not base my reaction on what I receive from others; that no matter how unjust, unfair, untruthful, unreliable, or unkind someone else is to me, I will not respond in a like manner.

And no matter how many times I have to put on and pull off someone's boots, I will still play nice. Because most of us are like this little boy—doing the best way we can with what we have!

Listen to Your Life

1. Who do you find it most difficult to play nice with? Name a type of person or a specific person.

2. What is it about that type of person or specific person that you find challenging?

3. What choices do you make right now about playing nice with that person?

Strategy 4: Relive When You Were There

Our daughter got her driver's license and within a couple of months did what most of us do—had her first accident. Now she's okay, but the car took a beating. And so did the board fencing around one of our horse pastures. She accidentally slammed into it going down our driveway, reaching for a too-important-at-the-time CD.

Every action has consequences. One of her consequences was helping me repair the fence one day. Now that meant digging up the old posts, re-digging the holes, planting new posts, measuring for and putting up new boards. Not exactly what every teenaged girl wants to do on a Saturday or their daddies for that matter, but it had to be done.

While we worked, we talked about the morning of her accident. She really was distraught, crying and apologizing over and over again, that morning. She was somewhat amazed that I didn't get any angrier than I did and wanted to know why.

That's when I told her about what flashed through my mind that morning as I stood there, surveying the damage—my first accident. I slammed a brand new Chevrolet Vega into an older Chevy Impala while learning to drive a manual transmission. The Vega was in reverse, and I couldn't seem to get the clutch and accelerator coordinated enough to take off without stalling. So my neighbor, who also happened to be our church's Minister of Music, told me to "Give it the gas and let off the clutch." I did and it all happened so quickly, I never knew how it happened. Fortunately, it was in his yard, on private property—just like her accident. I couldn't get too angry because I remembered mine.

You know, if you want to play nice, and listen to life with your spirit, it's best to remember your own humanity. Frankly, you are capable of anything that anyone's ever done before, and you may have actually done it before. Rather than berate our daughter for what she did, I remembered my accident, talked with her about what she could have done to prevent it, and provided the opportunity for her to repair the damages.

God gives you the grace necessary to remember your own humanity. It's a gift to your spirit from God's Spirit. So use it to play nice as you listen to life like a child and make a life, not just a living.

Listen to Your Life

1. What accident have you committed that you know someone else has done?

2. What did you learn that can benefit you in the future?

3. How will you share what you learned?

Strategy 5: Remember—It's Not All Yours

One clear, starry night, a family looked up at the stars. The little boy said, "Daddy, a boy in my class said the Big Dipper was in his backyard. I told him, 'No it isn't. It's in my back yard.' See, Daddy, there it is. I told him it was over my house."

The little boy's family tried explaining to him that the Big Dipper was in the sky which meant everyone could see it. He just couldn't understand how the Big Dipper could be over his house and over the other little boy's house, too.

So the little boy's mother said, "Think of the Big Dipper like God. God's at your house, God's next door and God's at that boy's house, too. If it is a clear night and someone looks up, they can see the Big Dipper, too."

The little boy thought for a moment, and then said, "Well Mommy, I know God is everywhere, but the Big Dipper is just over my backyard!"

Sometimes I act just like this little boy, don't you? I want it all for myself. I want to keep it all to myself. I don't want to share with anyone but myself.

Now I know this little boy's story may seem ridiculous to you, but how often do you act like him? Maybe not with the Big Dipper, but with something just as ludicrous—a possession of yours?

The hilarity of it all is that every single one of us is just passing through this part of the galaxy. You will not stay here forever. You are simply a steward of what's here for a brief time. So it can't all be yours. You will leave it behind for someone else.

So why not give some of it away? Why not share your Big Dipper, whatever it is, with someone else?

You'll discover that as you share and play nice, your Big Dipper becomes even larger, overflowing with the abundance of multiplied blessings, again and again recreating itself for you to share even more.

Remember—it can't all be yours. As you listen to life like a child, remind yourself of this truth and play nice.

Listen to Your Life

1. What possession is your Big Dipper, something you take pride in and really enjoy having?

2. What would be your response if God told you that you would have to give it up? Share part of it?

3. If satisfaction and contentment were animals, which ones would they be?

Strategy 6: Play Nice with Yourself

My brother called and was telling me about some of the antics of his son, my nephew. Joe was not quite two years old at the time and was really into "high-five's" then. Everyone he saw and knew, he greeted with "High-Five!" and a slap of the hands.

One evening, Joe ran from his room into the room with his parents. "High-five, Daddy!" he said and high-fived my brother. "High-five, Mommy!" he said and high-fived my sister-in-law. Then he just stood in the middle of the room, looking around for somebody else to high-five. Seeing no one, he thought for a moment and said, "High-five, Joe!" and high-fived himself and ran out of the room.

At some point in your life, you will run out of people to high-five in your home like Joe did. You will be alone, with no one to high-five, but that doesn't mean you have to be lonely. You see, where you are, God is with you. You may be alone, but you don't have to be lonely.

Recognizing that God is with you means that you look within yourself and there see and claim the proof that physically, you may be alone, but spiritually you don't have to be lonely. God's image and likeness are imprinted within you, in your spirit. As you close your eyes and see within yourself, there you discover God's creative purpose, your unique spiritual DNA, making you special and different from any of the billions of other people here.

For this reason, and so many manifestations of it, you can be alone without being lonely. You can give yourself a high-five and play nice with yourself. As you do, you listen to life like a child and make a life, not just a living!

Listen to Your Life

1. Who have you high-fived lately?

2. When was the last time you high-fived yourself? Can't remember? Then give yourself one now just because you are you!

3. Loving your neighbor as you do yourself is possible only when you love yourself. Make a list of qualities you love about yourself, seeing them as gifts from God.

Strategy 7: Ask Lots of Questions

Attending a wedding for the first time, a little girl whispered to her mother, "Why is the bride dressed in white?"

The mother said, "Because white is the color of happiness, and today is the happiest day of her life."

The little girl seemed satisfied with her mom's answer and sat quietly through the rest of the wedding until just about the very end. Then she leaned over to her mom again and whispered, "So why is the groom wearing black?"

Children have such a wonderful, natural curiosity about life and take nothing for granted, do they?

Somewhere along the way in growing up, I'll bet you stopped asking so many questions, didn't you? Now you just put your head down, keep shuffling your feet, speak when spoken to, try not to get in the way, go to bed, and get up the next morning to start all over again—doing the same thing, each day barely distinguishable from the previous.

You even stopped asking God questions, didn't you? You stopped wondering about a friend's suffering, or the color of rainbows, or how snowflakes can all be different, or what dogs are saying when they bark.

Where did that pure, innocent drive to wonder go? Do you know?

How long has your awe been subdued? Not sure?

Learning to listen to your life like a child is all about asking questions, some of them hard questions, and expecting answers from God. Not only is it about asking questions of God, it's also about learning to live with God's answers. Like this mother's answer, sometimes you get great answers from God, and other times, well, you file those answers under the "God is Infinite and I'm Finite" category.

If you truly desire to listen to life like a child, and want a much more fulfilling life through a personal relationship with God, start asking questions...again. You did it once when you were a child. Try it again!

Listen to Your Life

1. Take a walk on the next beautiful day. Keep your head up and look around as you walk. Ask lots of questions—"Why are bluebirds blue?" or something like that.

2. As you walk along, consider heavier matters of the heart. Ask God something about an event that occurred in your life.

3. Ask God to help you see life from more of God's perspective, and to give you the strength to live with the answers you hear...or don't hear.

Strategy 8: Let God in Your Heart

Have you ever been in a restaurant and it's obvious that children are in the place?

A friend who listens to life with us through www.listentolife.org emailed me about an experience he had in a restaurant. He and his wife were eating when a little girl, about four years old, came over to their table and just started talking with them.

"Hi! My name's Sarah. What's your name?" she said. My friend told Sarah their names and they talked for a while. Pretty soon Sarah drifted on over to another table and another and finally drifted back to my friend's table.

Our friend said, "Sarah, you sure are an energetic little girl. How do you stay out of trouble?"

And Sarah said, "I let God in my heart."

I guess at times in our lives, we're all energetic like Sarah. There's the potential you'll get into trouble. I mean, all of that energy has to go somewhere, doesn't it? And there are so many opportunities to channel energy down troublesome paths.

But Sarah understands how to listen to life, doesn't she? "I let God in my heart," she said. Once God is in your heart, you undergo a spiritual transformation. Suddenly, those troublesome challenges that once appeared so tempting fade into oblivion. The glitter and glitz of burning your energy in less than desirable ways holds no allure. Your spirit, touched by God's Spirit, now longs for profitable pathways not troublesome trails.

Join Sarah and stay out of trouble. Ask God to come into your heart and transform your spirit. Pray, "Don't lead me into temptation and deliver me from trouble." Then, and only then, are you ready to play nice as you listen to life and make a life, not just a living.

Listen to Your Life

1. What would you have said to Sarah had she walked up to your restaurant table?

2. How do you burn your energy?

3. Is God in your heart? How do you know? Think about your response to question 2 first.

Strategy 9: Connect

Our older daughter and I stood in line at a theme park, waiting to get on a ride. A girl about her age walked up behind us, wearing a T-shirt from the college I graduated from. My daughter noticed the shirt and said, "Hey Daddy! That shirt rocks. I'm gonna tell her!"

So she did. "Hi! I just wanted to tell you that your shirt rocks. My Dad went to that school."

At first, the girl didn't quite know what to say, but then she opened up: "Yea, it does rock. I hope to go there if I can get the financial aid I need."

I shared how I paid my way through the same college, working at a radio station a lot of hours every week, still took a full load of courses, and graduated on time. "So if I can do it, you can do it," I told her. "God has a plan for your life."

"I hope so," she said. And then she talked on and on about what she perceives is God's plan for her life. We asked her where she lives and she didn't think we would know her small town, but we did. And we just talked on until it was our turn to get on the ride.

You just never know, do you? When you get dressed in the morning, you just don't know who you'll run into that day and what will connect you with someone else. Something as innocent as a shirt can start a conversation with a stranger. And the conversation can turn to God.

But God knows. God knows all of the wonderful possibilities each new day holds in its tender caress. So as you dress in the morning and choose your clothes, know that even your clothes can connect you with another person. What you wear can help you play nice with others. What you put on in the morning can become a spiritual ritual as you ask God what to wear that day, not only so you can look as good as possible, but to connect you with others.

Connect with others today. It is a great way to listen to life like a child and make a life, not just a living.

Listen to Your Life

1. How do you select your wardrobe in the mornings?

2. Ever ask God what to wear? Why? Why not?

3. How can you connect today with someone you don't know?

Strategy 10: Talk So Others Understand

A teacher was testing the five and six-year old children in his class to see if they understood how to get to heaven. He asked them, "If I sold my house and my car, had a big garage sale and gave all my money to the church, would that get me into Heaven?"

"NO!" the children all answered.

"If I cleaned the church every day, mowed the yard, and kept everything neat and tidy, would that get me into Heaven?"

"NO!" the children all screamed.

"Well, okay then, if I was kind to animals and gave candy to all the children I know, and loved my wife, would that get me into Heaven?"

And again, they all answered, "NO!"

"Well," he said, "then how can I get into Heaven?"

And a five-year-old boy shouted, "You gotta be dead!"

Do you always communicate well? Or, like this teacher, do you know what you mean, but don't always consider how your listeners will hear what you say?

Of course, communication involves what you say, but not exclusively. In fact, most of communication is about your listener's background, preferences, and life experiences and your ability to relate what you have to say to those factors. The responsibility is yours as the one talking to communicate in a way that your listener can understand.

Then why do you get so frustrated with others when they can't understand you? Probably because it means you have more work to do, and who wants that, right? You want to be understood rather than try to understand your listener and phrase your words in such a way that they communicate well.

If you want to play nice in the world, if you want to share your spirit with others, work to understand who you're talking with more than trying to be understood. As you do, you'll be amazed at the transformation that takes place in your home, workplace, school, and other social settings. Listening to life like a child and making a life, not just a living is highly contagious!

Listen to Your Life

1. Recall the last time you had difficulty getting a family member, coworker, or friend to understand what you were saying. What was that experience like?

2. What could you have said differently to communicate better with that person?

3. How does God communicate best with you? When are you more likely to "get it" with God?

The End of the Beginning

Yes, I know, you're running out of pages, but, I promise, it's not the end. It's merely the end of your beginning.

That's right, you've begun a marvelous journey forward into the best years of your life by going backward. You're learning to listen to life like a child and to make a life, not just a living, the way God intends for you.

I want to help you continue your journey to listen to life. I want you to stay on this less-traveled road to make a life. So let me tell you how we can continue our journey together.

First, I've written other books. *Listen to Life: The First Book* and *Listen to Life, Too: The Second Book* are the first two books in this series. There are more books to come as well with one in the works that will include lots of great stories, but focus more on strategies than this book did. My working title is *The Secret of Life: A Six-Step Process to Listen to Life*. Find the page in the back of this book for how to order.

Second, if you'd like some daily inspiration, go to our website, www.listentolife.org. There you discover a FREE subscription to Today's Story. We'll send you an email every weekday and you get a great story from my own journey and people like you who share their stories with me.

Third, I do seminars and speaking engagements with folks all over the country. I'd love to meet you in person and talk with you about what you're continuing to learn about listening to life. Just email me at speaker@listentolife.org or click on the "Speaking" or "Seminars" link under "LIFE Resources" on our web site.

Fourth, I want to be your LIFE Coach, helping you along your life's journey from where you are to where you want to be—listening to life like a child and making a life, not just a living. Again, the web site contains all the info you need or you can call my office TOLL FREE at 1-877-4DRJOEY.

Fifth, you will want to take advantage of our LIFE Tele-seminars. From the comfort of your home, office, or favorite vacation spot, you call in and enjoy learning along with me and others as we have fun listening to life like a child. We tell stories, share strategies, and enjoy the journey together, like a learning community. Check out the details on our web site.

Finally, and there's lots more on our website, www.listentolife.org, I have a syndicated radio show and a syndicated newspaper column. It's the same story you get in your email daily, but it reaches so many people and it gives businesses who believe that listening to life and making a life, not just a living is important an opportunity to spread the goodness of this life transformation we're so blessed to be a part of.

All of that to say this: Congratulations! Your journey to listen to life has begun! And I want you to know that you're not alone in your travels. You have lots of companions on the trail. I've just named a few ways for you to stay connected, and who knows? There may be more developing between the time

I'm writing and you're reading this page. My hunch is there are...

...because you see, the journey is the destination. So I'll see you out there somewhere...on the road, listening to life.

(I'll be the one smiling and running and playing like a child!)

Acknowledgements

There are so many people who deserve to see their names on this page. I could write another book just listing them. Short of that, let me thank God. Give God the glory for whatever good this book accomplishes in your life and I'll take the blame for the mistakes. We're co-authors.

Next, let me thank my wife and daughters. My wife, with whom I share our daughters, is an incredibly patient and persevering life-partner who believes in me when I don't believe in myself. Thanks for loving me even when I act unlovable. And Rebekah and Elizabeth are two of the most incredible, uniquely gifted, passionate and playful daughters a Daddy could ever have. Thank you for teaching me how to be a child again and starting me down this path of listening to life and making a life, not just a living. Because of you two, I am alive.

Thank you also to my family, an amazing bunch of folks who, despite all of our foibles and faults, love each other all the time, like each other most of the time, and live with each other just some of the time now, but those times sure are sweet. Each of my ancestors contributed something unique, and I'm grateful to all of them, but especially to my parents who let me be a child.

There's one final person I want to acknowledge. The older I get the more I appreciate her influence on me. Starting in the fifth or sixth grade, Viola Babcock was my English teacher for three or four years. She taught me how to express myself properly through writing and speaking. She expanded my vocabulary, organized my writing, and taught me how to say "get" instead of "git," even while living in the South. Thank you, Mrs. B., wherever you are!

Discover the LISTEN TO LIFE Series Today!

Listen to Life Like a Child is Dr. Joey's latest book that coaches us to listen to life like a child and make a life, not just a living. Through everyday stories about experiences he's had with his daughters and other people with their children, this book revitalizes your spirit and connects you with the joyful Spirit of God. You listen to your life and hear God say:

- "Love You!"
- "Be Good"
- "Hold My Hand"
- "Look Both Ways"
- "Play Nice"

If you want to enjoy life like a child, this book is for you!

Listen to Life, Too: The Second Book is another wonderful, widely-acclaimed collection of everyday stories that you'll read over and over again. This book inspires you to make a life, not just a living and helps you focus on what's really important in life. It's just the book you want for living right now!

Listen to Life: The First Book is the widely-acclaimed first collection of everyday stories published by Dr. Joey. These inspirational stories are compiled from Dr. Joey's syndicated radio show, newspaper column and web site and expanded for your reading pleasure. They also include three "Listen to Your Life" reflection questions so that you can write your own stories about connecting with God's love.

Three Easy Ways to Buy the Listen to Life Series

1.   Call 1-877-4DRJOEY and place your order with one of our friendly associates who love talking with you, our friends.

2.   Go to www.listentolife.org 24/7 and order through our highly-secure, easy-to-use LIFE Resources Center. It's really that simple!

3.   Check your local bookstore. If they are sold out, have them order your copies today! We're available worldwide through the finest distribution network offered to booksellers.

If you have suggestions for more books in our Listen to Life series, email us at DrJoey@listentolife.org. If you'd like to share your Listen to Life stories with us, we're glad to receive them and may include them in our next book! Just go to www.listentolife.org and click on "Send Your Story."

If for some reason, you are not satisfied with any Listen to Life product or experience, we'll give you your money back, no questions asked.

Listen To Life Notes

Listen To Life Notes